READING THE SIGNS

POEMS BY JIM POTTS HAVE APPEARED IN THE FOLLOWING BOOKS:

Two point five edited by Tom Corbett, Victor French and Simon Heywood (London: The Poetry Society, London University Institute of Education, 1967).

16 Poems/16 Básní by Jim Potts, bilingual edition with Czech translations by Ladislav Verecký, Pavel Šrut and Ivo Šmoldas (Prague: Koháček & Trnka, 1989).

The Haiku Hundred edited by James Kirkup, David Cobb and Peter Mortimer (North Shields: Iron Press, 1992).

Swedish Reflections, from Beowulf to Bergman, edited by Judith Black and Jim Potts (London: Arcadia Books, 2003).

Corfu Blues by Jim Potts (Stockholm, Moscow & New York: Ars Interpres Publications, 2006).

The Cat of Portovecchio: Corfu Tales by Maria Strani-Potts (Blackheath NSW: Brandl and Schlesinger, 2007).

The Haiku 100 edited by Peter Mortimer, The Historic Collection (North Shields: Iron Press, 2015).

AND ALSO IN THE FOLLOWING PERIODICALS:

Ars Intrepres: International Journal of Poetry; *Translation and Art*; *Acumen*; *Cadences*; and the *William Barnes Society Newsletter*.

AND IN TRANSLATION IN:

Porphyras, Odos Panos, Endefktirio, Tomes, Ipeirotika Grammata and *O Phileleftheros* (Greek); *Calende: Revistă de cultură* (Romanian); *Lyrikvännen* (Swedish); and *Minimanimalia: Canzoniere Animinimalista di Raul Scacchi*, ed. Gioia R. Maestro Scacchi (Italian).

OTHER BOOKS BY JIM POTTS

The Ionian Islands and Epirus: A Cultural History (Oxford: Signal Books; New York: Oxford University Press; 2010).

This Spinning World: 43 Stories from Far and Wide (London: Colenso Books, 2019).

READING THE SIGNS

by

JIM POTTS

COLENSO BOOKS
2020

This collection first published February 2020 by
Colenso Books
68 Palatine Road, London N16 8ST, UK

ISBN 978-1-912788-06-4

Copyright © 2020 Jim Potts

The cover image is from a photo taken by the author.

"The city" was first published in *Two point five* (1967).

"The first lyre" was selected by Dannie Abse and read on BBC Radio 4 in *Time for verse* (2 September 1987).

"Gutenberg's first forty", "Maze of straw" and "Corfu haiku" were first published in *16 Poems* (1989).

"Corfu haiku" was republished in *The Haiku Hundred* (1992), *Corfu Blues* (2006) and *The Haiku 100* (2015).

"Outer Hebrides" was first published in *Swedish Reflections* (2003).

"Aloni", "Before the Paxos Beach Hotel", "Biodiversity", "Birth of love", "Cisterns", "Cult of the daisy", "Culture shock in Rome", "Delphic Oracle", "Dodona Oracle", "Dry-stone hideaway", "The first lyre", "From Ostrias Escarpment", "Gouvia morning", "In the far north", "Officer class", "Pavlosiko", "Paxos haiku", "Plaka, 2003", "Prika", a prose version of "Six hundred drachma per dolphin-nose", "Symphony of bells", "Thasos", "Vanda (1935–1951) and George", "Vanda's mother", and "Vitsa, after rain" were first published in *Corfu Blues* (2006).

"Dodona Oracle" and "Prika" were republished, and "Cats and rats", "Fish and fishermen" and "Seeing red" were first published, as epigraphs to chapters in the novel by the author's wife, *The Cat of Portovecchio* (2007).

"Arthur Rimbaud: the gates of Harrar" was first published in *Cadences: A Journal of Literature and the Arts in Cyprus* 9 (Fall 2013).

"May Day" was posted on ideoforein.blogspot.com (23 June 2018).

"If you're attentive . . .", "Song for Sherborne", "On leave after an illness", "Walking the coastal path from West Bay to Burton Bradstock" and "West Bay harbour" were posted on the William Barnes Society website, in "Some Dorset poems by Jim Potts" (williambarnessociety.org, November 2019).

For full publication details of the volumes referred to above, see the page facing the title page.

The other seventy-two poems in this collection are published here for the first time.

CONTENTS

The first lyre	1
Maiden Castle	2
On leave after an illness (at forty-five degrees)	2
West Bay harbour	3
West Bay	3
Walking the coastal path from West Bay to Burton Bradstock	3
Recurrent childhood memory	4
Maze of straw	4
Officer class	4
Confessions of a wanton schoolboy	5
Land reform (Second Hymn to Hugh MacDiarmid)	6
If you're attentive . . .	7
The city	8
Organic sandwich	8
Birth of love	9
Tsunami	9
Invalid	9
Conversation in the Quad (Oxford undergraduates overheard)	9
ALARA (on Winfrith, 1958–1990)	10
Global warming? "Poppycock!" — Professor David Bellamy CBE	11
After the wreck of the SS Torrey Canyon	12
Golfers v. Joggers	13
Back in Oxford at the Muses' Retreat	14
Song for Sherborne	16
Sweden, May 2002	16
Not yet midsummer	17
Everyman and Allemansrätten	17
Gotland	18
The somnabulist in Djurgården — the Orchard Archipelago, Rosendal Park	18
Sunday morning in Sweden	18
Sami joik	19
Viking haiku	19

CONTENTS

Seen at Skansen	19
Disorientation (Black Christmas, 2001)	19
Vltava, 1987	20
Gutenberg's first forty	20
Celebrating the Czech National Poet in 1987	21
Sartre's last words in La Rochelle	22
Culture Shock in Rome en route from Albania	22
In the far north	22
Biodiversity	23
Pavlosiko	23
Cats and rats	24
Fish and fishermen	24
Seeing red	24
Prika	24
Dodona Oracle	24
Corfu Crisis	25
May Day (*from the Greek of Vasilis Pandis*)	26
Vanda (1935–1951) and George	26
Vanda's Mother	26
Cult of the daisy	27
Gouvia morning	27
Karcharias	27
Cisterns	27
Corfu haiku	28
Winter days	28
Before the Paxos Beach Hotel	28
The Italian boy on Paxos	28
From Ostrias Escarpment	29
Paxos haiku	29
The bulldozers	29
Lapsed pantheist on Paxos	30
The bite of Freedom (Solomos and Strani)	30
Aloni	30
Plaka, 2003	31
After Dylan's "Desire"	31
Mouria and meltemi	32

CONTENTS

Skiathos: a fragment (1982)	32
Six hundred drachmas per dolphin-nose	33
Symphony of Bells (idiophones, in Halkidiki)	34
Thasos	36
Romiosyni: a postscript	36
A close call with a viper	37
Mediterranean	38
Sea view	39
Taken short	39
Vitsa, after rain	39
Dry-stone hideaway	40
Old Aristakis, Mount Gamila goatherd	41
Bliss disturbed	42
Squirrels and walnuts / Skiourakia ke karidia	43
Duet of nightingales	43
Petrohelidonia	44
Days apart: a double lament	44
Three plum trees	44
The Outer Hebrides (*from the Swedish of Eva Ström*)	45
The snake-charmer	46
Fulani flautist: nomad versus World Bank Agricultural Development Project	47
Ammonite	48
Trying to keep cool in Kano: a song	49
The cowrie shell: a song	50
Arthur Rimbaud: the gates of Harrar	52
Mooring at night by Maple Bridge (*from the Chinese of Zhang Ji*)	53
Coral reef	53
To Harry Wedge, on a bark by Mithinarri	54
Wandjina	54
Oh! brave white horses!	55
Strine haiku	56
Freedom	56
Strange fauna at Uluru (Ayers Rock)	58
Ficus benghalensis	59
Silversides, Bermuda	60

CONTENTS

Bermuda	60
Bermuda haiku	60
Blossom time, Washington DC	61
Blue Ridge Mountains	61
Noah's harp	61
A crime against humanity — Don't say we weren't warned	62
Hyacinthus orientalis	64
Delphic Oracle	65

READING THE SIGNS

As with the stories in Jim Potts' recently published collection *This spinning world* (Colenso Books, 2019), the poems in this volume reflect the many countries in which the author has lived and worked or which he has had reason to visit. The poems are arranged as a kind of journey — not a journey which reflects the course of Jim's life, for the basic principle of organization is geography and not chronology. We begin and end, though, with poems updating Greek mythology. "The first lyre", where the actions of Hermes and Apollo place poetry and song in a tense relationship with the natural world, is followed by poems set in England, especially in Dorset where Jim's principal home is. Then we move to Sweden, and from Sweden southwards through Europe, stopping briefly in Czechoslovakia (as it was called when Jim worked in Prague), then touching on France, Italy and Albania en route for Corfu, where we remain for several pages before moving to the nearby island of Paxos, and from there to various other locations in Greece, leading back to the mountains of Epirus, opposite Corfu. The translation of Eva Ström's "The Outer Hebrides" acts as a kind of farewell to Europe, and to the familiar, as the focus shifts to Africa, with poems set in Morocco, Nigeria, Kenya and Ethiopia. With a brief glance at China we move to Australia, with glimpses of its diverse cultures, and finally from there to Bermuda and the USA. The book ends with three poems set in no particular place: an angry cry summing up many of the concerns that inform these poems in "A crime against humanity", a ray of hope in the enigmatic "Hyacinthus orientalis", and a final warning in "Delphic Oracle" — these last two once again invoking Greek mythology, and the last taking a lead from a Greek epigram of the 4th century AD, often described as the last utterance of the Oracle at Delphi: "Tell the emperor that the hall so finely wrought has fallen down […] the water of prophecy run dry."

The first lyre

I know now when the Blues was born.

Once Hermes stumbled on a tortoise and he thought
"That's just what I've been looking for."
So he tore out its flesh with a chisel,
he emptied the shell, scraped the carapace clean —
a natural sound-box, but somewhat obscene.

What other animals did he not hesitate
to murder in the name of music?
He made two arms from the horns of a goat,
he stripped hide from an ox, stretched it over the shell.
He made seven strings from the guts of sheep,
and tautened them over a bridge.
He shaped a plectron of ivory, another of horn.
When he struck the strings, the sound was sweet.

As Hermes played, Apollo listened,
and at once his anger died.
But the animals howled and moaned —
not at all the Orphic effect.
Apollo accepted the gift of the lyre,
and composed a hymn of praise.

But the god of music
could not appease
the spirit of the tortoise.
The sheep-gut strings,
the wild goat's horns
and the skin of the ox
refused to serve his purpose.
He discovered the sound of a desperate Muse —
and Lyric Poetry was born with the Blues.

Maiden Castle,

Above the Roman Temple,
the skylarks sing,
redeem the *No-fly* spring.

*On leave after an illness
(at forty-five degrees)*

Gale-force winds on Maiden Castle,
my lungs, restored, blow full again.
Up and down the ancient ramparts
running, falling, with my son; then
leaning back against the wind —
invaders of the hillfort earthworks,
the grass swept wave-wild like our hair.
Dorchester spread out below us.

Thank God it's Hardy here, not Kafka.
On leave from Prague and airless office —
breathing deeply, inhaling Dorset,
the old tribal force and fortress-free.

West Bay harbour

West Cliffs
hang draped
like pleated curtains.

January moon
above Saint John's.

West Bay

Poised for attack, on guard, aggressive —
crabs' claws threaten.
The meat is sweet.

*Walking the coastal path
from West Bay
to Burton Bradstock*

Some people leap
from the top of sheer cliffs.
Others are buried
    by landslides.

Planned or unplanned,
life's all cliff-falls and ifs.

There's no saving hand.
Rocks erode, land subsides.

*Recurrent
childhood memory*

That mulberry tree.
The lazy stream. Midges.
Fish surfacing for food.

Maze of straw

We built a maze of straw-bales
in a Cornish farmer's field.
We crawled through on our bellies
but we found the exit sealed.

The way was dark and prickly,
we were lost, enclosed and scared.
With our backs we raised a roof-bale,
to face the farm-boy's sickle, bared.

Officer class

The voice of command
doesn't cut it round here.
Hark, the barking of dogs.

*Confessions
of a wanton schoolboy*

I murdered birds
when I was young.
I shot them with my gun
for fun
to feel the thrill of power.
Bluetit, chaffinch,
blackbird, starling,
a thrush, a linnet,
Robin Redbreast.
God forgive me.
Buddha too.

I slaughtered crabs
when I was young.
I found them cowering
under rocks.
I tortured them;
if they attacked,
pulled off their claws,
squashed in a back.
All this I can no longer hide.
God forgive my genocide,
and Buddha too . . .

Land reform
(Second Hymn to Hugh MacDiarmid)

Survey our green and pleasant land —
a patchwork of private estates!
Who owns the towns and counties?
Whose children inherit the Kingdom?
Dragons guard the secret vaults
where landlords count their acres;
the faceless few who own the farms
pore over one-inch Ordnance maps,
revise old boundaries,
enclose common fields,
set their seals on title deeds —
once the bribes of feudal barons.
Evicted tenants claw outside
at the bars and iron spikes —
the clamour of the dispossessed!
The landless sons of serfs and peasants
rise up to seize their birthright.
They leap over moats, over centuries,
they scale the walls and battlements,
ignoring the fences,
the hedges and ditches,
barbed-wire,
broken glass
and the dragon's breath —
now is the time for the battering-ram!
No power on earth can contain them . . .
Release us from rent and mortgage!
Redistribute the acres!
Land to the tiller!
To each an individual plot!
Lock up the landlords!
Confiscate their real estate!

Blow up the palaces, replace them with homes!
Burn the mansions and the manor-houses!
Demolish hotels and high-rise blocks!
Occupy offices, squat in the shops!
Level the highlands of the ruling class —
colonialists in their own country!
Disarm the men who shoot the grouse!
Take an acre of moorland, build your own house!
Liberate all the occupied land!
Peasants of the city slums,
now is the time for revolt!

The reason I'm writing this agitprop?
My great-grandfather owned an estate.
He had sixteen thousand acres
and a stately home to match.
Now that I need it, I don't even own
so much as a square inch of England.

All revolution is envy, revenge.
Don't talk to me of social justice.

> The subtitle of the poem evokes MacDiarmid's famous "Second Hymn to Lenin".

If you're attentive . . .
(April, near the Lulworth Ranges, Dorset)

Early bluebells
ring out in the woods,
muffle the shots from the firing range.

The city
(London, 1967)

A thousand hands
    wiped
upon a single towel.

A thousand smiles
    wiped
into a single scowl.

A thousand voices
    silenced
by one explosive vowel.

A thousand bodies
    collide.
Unheard the beggar's howl.

Organic sandwich

My *wheat-free organic-olive
dolphin-friendly* tuna sandwich
with *naturally-sun-dried tomatoes*
was somewhat hard to swallow.

It seemed to shout
"Discrimination!"

Birth of love

Though rooted in the scowling rockface
daisies break out,
smile at the sun.

Tsunami

Another seismic wave?
I plant wild primroses,
water the garden.

Invalid

Reduced to watching a single tree,
he's becoming
quite an expert.

Conversation in the Quad
(Oxford undergraduates overheard)

"My uncle died a rather ironical death."
—"Oh really; what happened?"
"He invented a fast-breeder nuclear reactor,
and he died of nuclear poisoning."

ALARA
(on Winfrith, 1958–1990)

In two to three years we've reduced part of the site from something that would kill you in a few hours to somewhere you can walk through in safety.
          Andy Staples, WOMAD
  (Winfrith Operations Maintenance and Decommissioning)
         BBC News Online, 30 April, 2004

Poole Harbour [...] contains radioactivity from Winfrith's liquid discharges and there is potential washout of gaseous discharges entering via the River Frome.
    CEFAS, *Radiological Habits Survey: Winfrith, 2003*

What should we say about Winfrith?
It's difficult to wax poetic
about the Steam Generating
Heavy Water Nuclear Reactor,
the plutonium laboratories on Egdon Heath,
the public's exposure to radiation,
the liquid radioactive waste
dumped in Weymouth Bay,
offshore of Arish Mell;
about the decommissioning and clean-up costs
of the contaminated hazardous heath,
the plans to restore the environment,
the drastic cuts to allocations.

Just two more reactors to go!

I read that the Nuclear Directorate
"will seek to focus a proportionate
level of regulatory attention
on ensuring the continued safety
of higher-hazard facilities."

The public's exposure to radiation
at least is only "ALARA"
(*As Low As Reasonably Achievable*).

I've asked Santa to bring me for Christmas
a sodium iodide scintillation detector.

Last year he brought me a Geiger counter.

Global warming? "Poppycock!"
— Professor David Bellamy CBE

"A climate-change denier",
"a global warming disbeliever",
a popular writer and presenter,
a botanist of note (surely no pariah) —
dropped, he claimed, from the BBC,
banished from the TV screen.
He believed in nature's cycles,
paid the price for his dissent.
He often came to Corfu
to lead botanic tours.
People loved his walks and talks.
Few spoke *then* of mass extinction.

David Bellamy died on 11 December 2019, aged 86.
This poem was written before his death.

After the wreck
of the SS Torrey Canyon
(Easter 1967)

the easter-bordered year
    is closed

the door
    is slammed

CONGRATULATIONS
    are telegrammed

we won
    the race

we played
    the game

the thick black oil
    invades the sands

with my own two hands
    I killed a gull

its white wings glued
    carrion-crowed

I was glad
    to see it die

forget the oil-slicks moving in —
let us take a moonlight swim

Golfers v. Joggers

It seemed like Somerset
instead of Muswell Hill
at six o'clock this morning.
The golf course was greenly glowing,
my shadow stretched for thirty feet
whichever way I jogged.
I was quite alone, without a care, unaware
of the two grim reapers taking aim.
Did they share the same love of lead-free air,
of moisture on grass in the morning?
Had they really come to play a game
or to drive off trespassers like me?
I heard a crack, but the ball fell short.
No one warned me, or shouted "Fore!"
When the second ball whizzed right past my ear,
my jogtrot turned to a desperate sprint.
I really began to run.
Of course they pay for their privilege —
they're members of the club. It is not a public park,
but nor are *they* landlords
of what meadows remain.
Joggers unite! Ignore the jeers.
You don't *have* to run round the North Circular Road.

Back in Oxford at the Muses' Retreat
(Wadham College, 14 December 1996)

All my past life is mine no more,
The flying hours are gone,
Like transitory dreams given o'er,
Whose images are kept in store
By memory alone.
    John Wilmot, Earl of Rochester

Hail Sacred Wadham! whom the Muses Grace,
And from the rest of all the Reverend Pile
Of Noble palaces, design'd thy Space
Where they in soft retreat might dwell,
They blest thy Fabric, and they said — do Thou
Our Darling Sons contain;
We Thee our Sacred Nursery ordain,
They said, and Blest, and it was so . . .
    Aphra Behn

> The only surviving tree from Shipley's time is the enormous but declining copper beech (girth 18′8″ 1992), planted when it was a novelty. By 1905, *Country Life* considered it "the finest in England" and it had a girth of 11′6″ in 1912.
>   D. J. Mabberley, "The Gardens", in *Wadham College* (1994)

> It was felled and the root dug out in 1995, which is when it reached its Bicentennial. There was some talk at the time of reducing the tree to make it safe and trying to keep it, but to be honest it was very badly infected with Honey Fungus which would have killed it in a few years. It also had a bracket fungus called *Ganoderma* which destroys the heart wood of the tree, so I'm afraid it had a very limited amount of time left. It had started to shed branches in the summer [...] Next time you visit College you might be interested to see a young Beech in the Fellows' Garden which is planted closer to the Chapel; this is a seedling of the old Beech, which I grew from seed. It is now about 25 years old and is looking very fine.
>   Andrew Little, Head Gardener, email 27 November 2019

I've just flown in from Sydney.
It's wintertime again.
The porter at the college lodge,
laments the fate of the old copper beech:
"The tree surgeon said
Cut it down, there's no hope."
Two hundred years old,
they say it looked sickly before it was felled.
It shed some of its branches.
There was no sign of root-rot

or beech-bark disease,
but it bore Honey Fungus and *Ganoderma*.
It was only after the bonfire
that blame was being laid
on those who'd hated the copper beech,
"That ornamental novelty tree!"
Others joined in with a belated lament:
"Alas, the old copper beech tree —
if only it could have been saved."

Some beech nuts had been gathered,
So all was not lost.
"Beechmast for strong saplings,"
the Head Gardener said.
He tenderly planted some seed from the tree.
His seedling has thrived, it grows close to the Chapel
in the Fellows' Garden, where I'd lie down and read.
Soon I'll return to express overdue thanks,
remembering old friends, some long since dead,
to see again copper leaves set bright against green,
repeating words that I once studied there:
"After-comers cannot guess the beauty been."

> The last line is a quotation from Gerard
> Manley Hopkins' "Binsey Poplars".

Song for Sherborne
(In Old English Scir Burne meant "clear stream")

I went down to Sherborne Town
looking for that crystal stream.
I asked Saint Aldhelm, but he replied,
"Things are never what they seem."

> It's a muddy stream,
> it's a murky lake,
> and those water rats
> are all wide awake.

I searched and searched to find the source
where the babbling brook was bright and pure.
Each step I went, the water's course
seemed much less clear and far less sure.

> It's a muddy stream,
> it's a murky lake,
> and those water rats
> are all wide awake.

Sweden, May 2002

Dandelions, daisies, daffodils,
violets and forget-me-nots.
all the trees in blossom,
birds in full song.
Sweden is Eden
this amazing May.

Not yet midsummer

I'd forgotten the forget-me-nots.
The fields are full of them
this early Swedish summer,
the copses, the clearings,
the churchyards. How
beautiful they look — that life-enhancing blue
all around the headstones.

Everyman and Allemansrätten
(Galberget, Visby, Gotland)

I like this right of public access,
Allemansrätten, Everyman's Right,
which allows us to enjoy
"the fragrance of flowers,
the singing of birds,
the silence of the forest,
the flower-covered meadows" —
to swim in the sea,
to sail in all waters,
to tie up our boats,
to wander ashore,
to walk across land,
pick berries and mushrooms,
wild flowers for our wreaths:
Midsummer Night's lovers,
unmindful of loss.

Gotland

What did I get from Gotland?
Fine walls, wild flowers
and towers of stone.

*The somnambulist in Djurgården —
the Orchard Archipelago, Rosendal Park*

"Troubled skies and crashing waves" —
Strindberg's favourite subjects,
when walking to Rosendals Trädgård,
from Karlaplan or Drottninggatan,
eyes fixed firmly straight ahead,
dreaming Kymendö and Sandhamn
(Runmarö, Dalarö, Furusund, Huvudskär)?
Trees as symbols of the wild, high seas.

Karlaplan and Drottninggatan are streets where Strindberg lived; the names that follow are some of his favourite islands in the Stockholm archipelago.

*Sunday morning
in Sweden*

By the River Ume,
rain clouds overhead:
grey-black or *silver-blue?*

Sami joik

A reindeer drive
on the river ice.
Fifteen hundred, with their herders.

A *joik* is a traditional form of song among
the Sami, with its own style of vocalization.

Viking haiku

Food for the eagle,
the raven, the wolf.
Better all these, than the worm.

Seen at Skansen

She's like a slim, young elk-calf
lying, stretching,
in the autumn sunshine.

Skansen is an outdoor museum in Stockholm where traditional
buildings from all over Sweden have been reconstructed.

*Disorientation
(Black Christmas, 2001)*

Bush-fires rage round Sydney.
In Stockholm, snow-flakes fly.
Where on earth am I?

Vltava, 1987

The Vltava is a river
for sad painters,
doomed lovers,
unprotesting protest-singers,
melancholic poets,
regretful revolutionaries,
compromised composers.
It succumbs to the planners
and jumpers from bridges.
We get the rivers we deserve.

Gutenberg's first forty

Forty printed parchment Bibles:
a giant step for Man.
For forty Bibles
ten thousand sheep.

Does God count them
    in his sleep?

Celebrating the Czech National Poet in 1987

For Hugh Hamilton McGoverne, translator of *Máj*
and instigator of readings in both Czech and English
at the statue of Mácha in Prague, 1946–1949.

By the statue of Mácha
Czech lovers were standing,
sharing in silence soft moments of twilight,
late in the evening, the first day of May.
Young couples, old couples,
offering flowers and laying their love-wreaths,
dandelion necklaces, daisy-chain rings,
adorning their poet on Prague's Petřín Hill.
The blossoming trees wooed all the lovers,
the fragrant flowers breathed moist sweetness at dusk.
Like an altar of love, the disciples adoring,
applauding their poet for the language he used:
"Květoucí strom lhal lásky žel".

The last line is the 6th line of the first canto of
Máj (May), a book-length romantic poem (1835)
by Karel Hynek Mácha (1810–1836). It means
"The blossoming tree belied the pain of love".

Sartre's last words in La Rochelle

In La Rochelle he lost his faith.
Those were the worst years of his life.
But, ah, those existential oysters —
(a toast to their Creator)
with a *Pineau des Charentes*!

Pineau des Charentes is an aperitif, a fortifed wine produced in western France, where the Atlantic port city of La Rochelle is located.

Culture shock in Rome en route from Albania
(June 1992)

Parma ham served with melon and figs —
after a week in Tirana!
No wonder they rushed to take ship at Durres,
ignored the barbed-wire surrounding the dockyards,
clung to old tyres and put out to sea.
We found lop-sided rafts, capsized by a breeze.
They're breaking down their bunker-thinking
but all they get is food for thought.

In the far north

The first fire-flies in Corfu!
The sweet smell of jasmine
Reaches me here.

Biodiversity

"Non-native
invasive
biodiversity" —
we're being warned about it
by a boffin on the radio.
A global threat,
a deadly danger.
That means me,
when I first set foot in Corfu
(or in the Southern Continent).
Not just the bugs
on the soles of my shoes.
Non-native
invasive
biodiversity —
a fancy name.
I fit the bill.

Pavlosiko
(in an open market in Corfu)

I love to stop
for a prickly pear
peeled by the man christened "Cactus".

Cats and rats

Which do you want,
the rats or cats?
Poison the one, you kill the other.

Fish and fishermen

Young girls gaze at fishermen with nets:
the cats are all eyes
for the fish.

Seeing red

The Old Port, the slaughterhouse —
the sea runs red
where children swim in blood.

Prika

Her only dowry was the sea,
the best a man could have.
An empty chest. Her only dowry
the sea, the unspoilt sea!

Dodona Oracle

The leaves are not rustling,
The pigeons don't fly —
Wild flowers are saying
"You'll live till you die."

Corfu Crisis

What have they done?
Where has all the rubbish gone?
Have they burned it, interred it,
forbidden it, hidden it,
sent it abroad
for others to hoard,
to sort or incinerate,
dispose of any old way they will?

Is that a real hill
or a hole that they fill
every day with the swill
and the rotting detritus,
the plastic and packaging
which stays there to blight us
(which we all buy in haste)
— not forgetting the hospital waste.

But at last (and at least)
it's not lining the streets,
nor polluting the fields and ground water.
If it's all being recycled
(either sold or recycled) —
then Bravo! *Bravo paidia!*

paidia: literally "children", but also the equivalent of the unisex use of "guys" when addressing people

May Day
(from the Greek of Vasilis Pandis)

The First of May, the grey skin of a snake
shed deep in the gardens of Mon Repos,
near the paths where the thrushes sing —

over there, hidden in the balmy undergrowth,
the naked snake
lies in wait for me.

Mon Repos with its extensive gardens to the south of Corfu
Town is the former summer palace of the Greek royal family.

Vanda (1935–1951)
and George

Blissful swimming
in Corfu seas.
A secret love-tryst.
Just her luck
to meet a straying shark.

(Witnessed by Naki Tsepeti, from Mon
Repos Jetty, 12 noon, 17 August 1951)

Vanda's mother

All the shutters of the house
stayed closed.
She couldn't bear to see the sea.

Cult of the daisy
(Corfu)

Lying amongst olive trees
and long-stemmed daisies,
I'm counting my springs.

Gouvia morning

Donkeys, dogs, cockerels,
swallows, soon cicadas!
The sounds around us.

Karcharias

Somewhere the shark is waiting.
In the shallows? In the shadows?
Hungry.

Carcharias is a genus of sand tiger shark, but in Greek *karcharias* is a general word for "shark".

Cisterns

Cisterns, wells and threshing floors:
before Poetry,
the fundamentals.

Corfu haiku

Twenty-one dolphins
danced in the harbour.
The teacher kept on talking.

Winter days

The halcyon days are over.
Waves grow wild again —
seabirds seek land.

Before the Paxos Beach Hotel

We camped there thirty years ago —
down on that olive terrace.
We swam down in that pebbly bay
avoiding sharp sea urchins.
I'm living in Australia,
you're in Canada, they say.
I still see our tent in the olive grove,
a faint impression where we lay.

The Italian boy on Paxos

The boy dropped the tortoise
into the bay
to see if it turned turtle.

From Ostrias Escarpment
(looking down at the new road
to Avlaki Creek, Paxos)

They've opened a road
below my secret perch —
a gash across my heart.

Paxos haiku

With sixty-four churches
to choose from, there's no need
to feel all is lost.

The bulldozers

The bulldozers
are busy on Paxos,
waiting to ravage
more pathways,
to tear down terraces,
dry stone walling,
to uproot olive and cypress,
the carob tree, myrtle and pine
out towards cape, cliff and headland,
hidden cove and well-loved lookout.
The bulldozers
are busy on Paxos.
Ripping out roots, they advance.
The bulldozers are getting more greedy,
the ground-grabbers,
the merchants of scars.

Lapsed pantheist on Paxos

Crystal water — urchins — sharks?
Nature's Bounty.
That vast indifference.

The bite of Freedom
(Solomos and Strani)

Blame the mosquitoes
For *The Hymn to Freedom*.
They drove Dionysios out of his house
To seek peace on the Hill of Strani!

The Hymn to Freedom (1823) by Dionysios Solomos (1798–1857) is a long poem about the Greek War of Independence, (1821–1829). It was on the Hill of Strani (named after Solomos's friend Ludovico Strani, who lived there) on the island of Zakynthos, that Solomos began the composition of the poem. In the 1860s the first three (later the first two) of its 158 4-line stanzas were adopted as the Greek national anthem.

Aloni

As hard as marble, copper, iron,
the threshing floor
where Charon waits.

Plaka, 2003

Watching the tourists
come traipsing down from the Acropolis
I don't think they look
like their lives have been changed.
They're glad to flop down
in a shady taverna
with a plateful of squid, in Plaka.
There are always more marbles.
*Finite,
the fruits of the sea.*

Plaka is an old district of Athens, with narrow streets, on the slopes of the Acropolis.

After Dylan's "Desire"

One more glass of ouzo
'fore I go —
where starfish and sea-urchins grow.

Compare the refrain of one of the songs on Bob Dylan's album *Desire* (1976): "One more cup of coffee / 'fore I go / to the valley below".

Mouria and meltemi
(Nimborio, Andros)

Under the mulberry trees of Chora.
The sea is not as smooth as silk.
The wind gusts hard at Beaufort 7.
White horses rear up around the rocks.
The lighthouse sails towards the shore.
Hungry cats crack chickens' wing-bones.

mouria: mulberry trees
meltemi: a strong dry north wind in the Aegean, May–September
Chora: a generic name for the chief town on a Greek island

Skiathos: a fragment (1982)

The sea was thick as pasta soup,
with jellyfish, both big and small.
What worse was washed up on the beach?

Bags and bottles, flip-flops, potties,
limbs of dolls and flotsam toys.
A plague upon this plastic waste!

Ajax! Most flotsam bottles aptly labelled.
The contents may have cleaned a house —
the containers foul the ocean.

*Six hundred drachmas
per dolphin-nose*
(Ouranoupolis, Halkidiki, 1983)

Henceforth
fewer fishing nets
need be torn.
Dolphins are outlawed.
No longer friends to fishermen,
now pests, not friends to men —
no more to play near ships, near shore;
their developed dolphin language
does not undo
the damage to the nation's nets.
*Any dolphin brought ashore
will have its nose
chopped off.*
The competent authorities
have proclaimed it so.
No fisherman
should present for payment
the same dead dolphin twice.
The severed nose prevents abuse.
Six hundred drachmas per dolphin-nose.
The Ministry of Agriculture
must protect the fishing industry.
The Department of Wildlife Conservation
has declined to offer comment.

Symphony of Bells
(idiophones, in Halkidiki)

If I could have recorded
the concert of goats' bells
chiming and pealing, as the herd moved along,
tuned to each other, harmoniously tinkling,
nothing else would I listen to
all my life long.

    Out of two hundred, out of two hundred
    out of two hundred none rang a note wrong.

Some were pitched deeply and others pitched higher,
true perfect notes, tuned octaves apart.
and the goatherd he chivvied, coaxed and conducted,
and his calls to the herd were sweeter than song.

    Sweeter than song, sweeter than song,
    and his calls to the herd were sweeter than song.

Shimmering sound among the red poppies,
clanging with crimson in pastures of green;
goats of all shades of black, white and brown,
on the track through the dunes, right down by the sea.

    Down by the sea, down by the sea,
    clinking and tinkling down by the sea.

The goatherd's family followed the herd,
wife and two children, the field was their school.
Virgilian vision, Theocritan idyll,
Such miraculous music brings it back to us still.

The dangling bells of the billy-goats donged,
and the kids, keeping up, made double the dings.
The pattern of sound was sequenced and planned,
the composer was pulling invisible strings . . .

Pastoral symphony, magical music,
music for magic, to ward off evil eye:
eye of the tourist, caught behind camera,
eye of the Cyclops, and caster of spells,
eye of the herdsman within the next valley,
covetous goatherd, possessing few bells.

    Out of two hundred, out of two hundred,
    out of two hundred, none rang a note wrong.

        He-goats and she-goats,
        she-goats and he-goats,
        bucolic notes
        of bells within bells.

Thasos

Like Archilochos
I came to Thasos,
but saw no *savage* woods.
Just trees,
blue seas,
rows of hives
and honey bees.

Archilochos was a Greek poet
of the 7th century BC.

Romiosyni: a postscript

Αὐτὰ τὰ δέντρα δὲ βολεύονται μὲ λιγότερο οὐρανό
These trees cannot be accommodated under a lesser sky
                                Yannis Ritsos, *Romiosyni*

They're knocking down another house,
they're cutting down another tree;
they clear the forest in the night,
do as they please, without a right.

They're offering their village plots
in exchange for flats in concrete blocks.
They encroach on conservation zones,
bulldoze graveyards, grandparents' bones.

They're destroying the wildlife, hunting turtles and birds,
they dynamite fish, then deny it: fine words.
They're ready with fencing to claim newly-cleared land.
the *agrofilakas* knows; he too lends a hand.

They steal a *stremma* of woodland when nobody looks...
And nobody looks when pockets are filled,
and nobody questions, or audits the books,
and laws are not drafted, or they're never enforced.

Romiosyni? — *Rayadosini!*

Demolish all trace of tradition —
live under your lesser sky!

> *agrofilakas*: a rural policeman (literally "field guard")
> *stremma*: a unit of land area = 1,000 square metres
> *Romiosyni*: Greekness, the spirit of Greece or Greeks
> *Rayadosini*: slave mentality

A close call with a viper

The viper that lives in the old stone shed
tried to bite me today, I could have been dead.
I lifted a slab, he aimed for my hand.
I'm not ready to join that old angel band.

Mediterranean
(Thermaic Gulf, 1981)

Poisson pourri de Salonique. Rotting fish of Salonica.
Ta mère fit un pet foireux. Your mother a did a sloppy fart.
  Guillaume Apollinaire, "Réponse des Cosaques Zaporogues . . ."

Bloated mullet
float upturned at the water's edge,
gills and gullet
glutted with filth.

The sea is like shit-soup tonight.
The crap floats on top
like croutons.
Ti orea!

Unsinkable contraceptive sheaths,
undulating squid-like shrouds,
exotic seaweed, little streamers,
wound round rotting crabs and fish,

flushed with all the effluent
down countless pipes
from elegant apartments
along the *paralia*.

Those who wore them
in the heat of the night
disown them in the day.
They sit and sip their ouzos,
admire the misty peak of Olympus
across the wine-dark bay.
Ti orea!

Ti orea!: How nice!   *paralia*: sea-front

Sea view

Who needs a sea view?
They're all in my mind's eye,
each harbour, bay and beach.

Taken short

Your heart could stop
at any time.
Better smell those roses.

Vitsa, after rain

Clear, bright morning in the mountains.
Sheeps' bells —
and honey in my yoghurt!

Dry-stone hideaway
(Vitsa, 1983)

Before I came I'd had the dream,
A cobbled path, a *kalderim*,
leading down the mountainside
to a high-arched bridge, an ice-cold stream.

The village houses, split mountain rock,
flagstone slabs to slate the roofs,
the cistern in the high-walled yard.
Water pure, of melted snow, the shaft well-made,
made long ago, eggshell-coated, calcium-sealed.

Arches and a cosy hearth. Wooden platforms for a bed.
A hideaway in Epirus; landscape such as Byron loved.
An Englishman's dream of home in Greece.
Children's voices, the cattle-bells.
Rectangles and curves.
Grey stone and white *flokati*.
We're roughly dressed, at one with stone.
The log-fire roars, it spits and burns,
it dies, leaps back to life in turns.
We pass our time in tending it,
cracking walnuts, toasting bread.
The water in the cauldron boils;
bright copperware reflects the flames.
Though the snow-wind whistles over beams,
through holes in roof and walls and floor,
the glowing cinders keep us warm:
they'd glow all night in glad *mangali*,
we'd sleep by it, if not for fumes.

We huddle round hearth and aproned fire
and bake potatoes in their skins.

Before all embers turn to ash,
it's time for twentieth-century sins:
switch on the electric blankets!

We pray no mouse will gnaw the wire.
We shall not dream of wolves, of bears.
As modern peasants we retire,
a family at peace, content.
Unique, the quality of quiet: monastic *isihia*.
We hear the basil breathe and grow,
wake with cattle-bells, cockerel's crow.

Canyon or gorge?
With its forests and flora,
Vikos invites us to return in the spring,
when wild flowers flourish on the threshing floors!
We resolve to learn their names next year.

kalderim(ia): well-constructed stone-built paths found throughout
Greece, many dating from the Ottoman or even Byzantine periods
flokati: handmade woollen tufted rugs
mangali: portable bowl-shaped metal charcoal brazier for heating
a room
isihia: peace, silence, rest

*Old Aristakis,
Mount Gamila goatherd*

They call him *Lord of the Gorge*.
Alone with his goats
on vertical slopes.

Bliss disturbed

Sitting in the shade
of the old walnut tree
at the bottom of the orchard,
gazing at the mountains,
listening to bird-song,
the buzzing of the bees,
the drone of the insects,
the barking of a dog:
the quiet hum of nature.
Thinking of threshing-floors.
Re-counting our cash
to see — will it last? —
if the banks don't reopen,
the ATMs won't put out;
if political chaos
disrupts normal life.

A peaceful existence,
with the shelves nearly empty,
no fuel for the car?

And down in the orchard
we've picked the last cherries . . .

Written in Vitsa, a village in the Zagori region of Epirus, northwestern Greece, two days before the Greek referendum of 5 July 2015, held to determine whether Greece should accept the financial bailout terms offered by the "Troika" (European Commission, International Monetary Fund and World Bank). The outcome was "No", but the Prime Minister resigned and, after a period of "political chaos", a new government renegotiated the deal and the bailout took place.

Squirrels and walnuts / Skiourakia ke karidia
(for Frixos Tziovas, Vitsa, September 2016)

Squirrels are jumping in our walnut tree.
They leap among leaves, from branch to branch.
They've gnawed and nibbled all our nuts,
bored and drilled, left shells with holes —
part-payment for their filling meals,
for a tree's supply of food that's free?
We gather the few that fall intact,
for a Christmas stocking, for the kids to crack.
We may make *gliko tou koutaliou* —
one jar at most.
Efcharistoume, skiourakia!
Orea, ta karidia mas?

gliko tou koutaliou: "spoon sweet", preserved fruits
(or nuts) in syrup. The last two lines mean "Thank
you, squirrels! Are they nice, our walnuts?"

Duet of nightingales

Almost dusk in the garden yard,
a nightingale trills its heart out.

I fetch my iPad, search the Net,
and start a thrilling singing bout!

Petrohelidonia
(June 2011)

House martins, stone-swallows
make their nests above our cistern.
Welcome home!

Petrohelidonia, literally "stone-swallows"
is the Greek for house martins.

Days apart: a double lament

Two baby swallows
fell out of their nests
under the eaves of our house

Three plum trees

Without even asking,
she cut down two plum trees
to make the third grow stronger.
But it isn't the fruit that I miss:
I loved the shade they all made.
Now my hammock has nowhere to hang —
And I'll be dead by the time
there's shade again for my head.

The Outer Hebrides
(from the Swedish of Eva Ström)

If it's the case that you long for the Outer Hebrides
or somewhere else, where you have the sea in front of you
and Europe behind you
and where the islands are only a thin film of rain . . .
If it's the case, that you're yearning for these islands
or other islands, of comparable unimportance . . .

If it's the case that you're worn out with writing Encyclopaedias
and reading them from A to Z . . .
If you've absorbed all the knowledge that there is to be acquired
about the Jarrah forests and the Druids,
about Tantalus on to the Tatras . . .
And if it's the case that the azaleas are fading
that their swollen pink petals have already dried
and dropped to the ground
and nothing is left of their hardiness,
their relationship to Ericacea, the heather on the moor —
hot-house flower, green-house flower . . .

If it's the case that you sense inside you the end is coming,
like a crack, or an idea emerging . . .
If it's the case that you long to be changed while you travel,
just as unripe fruit is changed as it travels
in the cargo-hold, beneath the Southern Cross,
a hull's-width away from the water . . .

If that's the case and there's no other option —
if that's how it is —
you've already turned off the lights in the house:
                you're on your way.

The snake-charmer
(Tangier, 1964)

In the Kasbah
a voice is heard to drone
and the strings of a *gunibri*
sing —

the young men grow mute
as they hear what is spoken:

"The charmer of snakes
has broken her flute,
her charm, too, is broken —
the snakes have awoken —
and one by one they stiffen,
and sting."

Fulani flautist: nomad versus World Bank
Agricultural Development Project
(Gombe, Nigeria, September 1978)

At the edge of the forest reserve
we stopped to stretch our legs.
The road gangs had not reached this far.
The jungle cats had yet to come
to claw up trees and undergrowth.
No bulldozers, graders or scrapers,
no pipeline crews; only our Landrover
had so far disturbed the peace.
Out of the forest the faint sound of a flute,
a mirage of silver-white cows.

I watched the herd materialise,
the sound of the flute grew louder.
Long-horned cattle, groomed like stallions,
sleek-skinned, clean and cared-for.
The Fulani flautist emerged from the trees,
standing before us with a welcoming smile.
He stopped to play, acknowledged our interest,
and them ambled away with his herd.

I would have followed the Fulani herdsman,
but I could hear less soothing sounds.
The big yellow cats were coming,
rumbling through the forest reserve.
The ground was beginning to tremble
and the fragile flute of the nomad
would soon be crushed beneath caterpillar tracks,
and the cattle would soon have to graze
on whatever might be left
between the asphalt and acres of maize.

Ammonite
(Ashaka, Bauchi State, Northern Nigeria)

I have a mind to meditate tonight:
so talk, triassic ammonite!
I discovered you just as you lay
where the first dinosaurs used to play —
two hundred million years ago?
You lived long before the plants had flowers
or so my book informs me.
Coil-like creature, you've survived so long.
How could anyone cut you in half?
You were not meant to be an ornament.
You watch me with mild amusement
as I approach my middle age.
Me? No, I'm not mesozoic —
but sometimes I feel like a fossil.

Trying to keep cool in Kano: a song

I've got no sense of direction,
I don't know which path I should choose.
I'm just trying to keep cool in Kano.
Last week I had snow on my shoes.

The roads were all blocked by the blizzards,
I half hoped I might miss the flight,
but as soon as I checked in they grabbed me,
they strapped me in for the night.

So I'm back with the dust and the lizards,
open drains and gastric despair.
Why did I ever leave Dorset,
green fields and that smell of sea-air?

I'm deep in the North of Nigeria,
the harmattan's blowing today.
They've never seen a homesick snowman —
they won't mind if I just melt away.

The Hause live in mud houses,
which sometimes collapse in a flood.
I want to get back to my missus,
you can't raise a mortgage on mud.

I travel to pay for my pleasures,
so they send me wherever they choose.
They treat me like some kind of cargo:
if I don't make it she'll hear on the news.

The cowrie shell: a song
(Mombasa, 1976)

I was a creature lost in a crevice,
you were a shell displayed on the reef.
I was the hermit crab seeking a home,
you were a cowrie washed up by the sea.

    Cowrie shell, cowrie shell out on the reef,
    cowrie shell coloured bright, beyond belief.
    Cowrie shell, cowrie shell, let me come in
    I'm just a poor hermit, with such a thin skin.

Come in, said the cowrie, and don't make me weep —
a collector may come by, and take me to keep.
Or a swordfish will eat you, so you'd better hide —
what a life for a lover to be cowering inside.

    Cowrie shell, cowrie shell out on the reef
    Cowrie shell coloured bright, beyond belief.
    Cowrie shell, cowrie shell, let me come in
    I'm just a poor hermit, with such a thin skin.

Cowrie shell, cowrie shell out on the reef,
Cowrie shell coloured bright, beyond belief.
We'll find a quiet coral pool, we'll call our own,
We'll hide under seaweed or under a stone.

    Cowrie shell, cowrie shell out on the reef
    cowrie shell coloured bright, beyond belief.
    Cowrie shell, cowrie shell, let me come in,
    I'm just a poor hermit, with such a thin skin.

Oh no, said the cowrie, such a life would be hell.
Let me lie in the sun, to show off my shell
or my colours will fade, I'll suffer such grief.
Leave me here on the coral, admired on the reef.

> Cowrie shell, cowrie shell out on the reef,
> cowrie shell coloured bright, beyond belief.
> Cowrie shell, cowrie shell, let me come in
> I'm just a poor hermit, with such a thin skin.

I'll leave you alone, and find a faded old shell.
I'll never forget you, but I'm wishing you well.
I hope you'll be happy inside a glass case.
I'd choose the blue ocean for my resting-place.

> Cowrie shell, cowrie shell out on the reef,
> cowrie shell coloured bright, beyond belief.
> Cowrie shell, cowrie shell, let me come in
> I'm just a poor hermit, with such a thin skin.

To be washed by the waves, to be watched by the fish,
but to die a true hermit, that is my wish.
Cowrie shell, cowrie shell out on the reef
Here comes an admirer, so wink at the thief!

Arthur Rimbaud: the gates of Harrar

From the mountains of Troodos
to the hills of Entoto
and down to the Ogaden,
from Soho to Shoa is not very far,
if you've passed through the gates of Harrar.

I met him once in Cyprus,
he just laughed and asked after Verlaine.
I met him again in Harrar,
crying out with a crippling pain.
I met him for the last time in France,
after he'd lost his leg.

"Never again will I ride a horse,
never again shall I spin or dance.
Oh take me back to Harrar,
where I shall not have to beg,
amber and musk must be cheap there now.
I'll make a fortune, then take a wife,
I'll have a son, and teach him all I've learned of life . . ."

From the mountains of Troodos
to the hills of Entoto
and down to the Ogaden,
from Soho to Shoa is not very far,
if you've passed through the gates of Harrar.

Mooring at night by Maple Bridge
(from the Chinese of Zhang Ji
on a calligraphy roll bought in Beijing)

The moon is setting; the cawing of crows.
Cold air. Frost's coming.

A fisherman's lamp hangs on the boat.
Frosted late autumn leaves above him,
a stranger tries to sleep: sad thoughts.

From Hanshan Temple outside Gusun City
comes the continuous sound of a bell at midnight,
reaching the stranger's boat. Pitch blackness.

Coral reef

The coral reef is crumbling
like my life:
reduced to rubble.

To Harry Wedge, on a bark by Mithinarri

"You don't know nothing about us"
— that's the title of his work I bought.
It's true, Harry, I admit it. But I'm trying.
Have you ever been to Arnhem Land?
I can't tell an ancestral file snake
from a Rainbow Serpent or sacred olive python.
Is that *bäpi* or the *wititj* totem?
I've never been to Garrimala
in Galpu Country, to which this bark
alludes, according to my catalogue.
But I can praise, appreciate.
I'll learn to say, when I'm no longer in the dark,
"Him bin do alright that bark."

A "bark" is a painting made on the inside of a piece
of tree bark — an important Indigenous Australian
art form.

Wandjina

    Mamadai and Wanalirri
    where *Wandjina* shelter —
    god-like faces on rock and cave.
    Mouthless image of creator —
    round eyes on bark, on canvas, slate
    make the rains come soon, come late.

Oh! brave white horses!

Oh! brave white horses! you gather and gallop,
The storm sprite loosens the gusty reins;
Now the stoutest ship were the frailest shallop
In your hollow backs, or your high arch'd manes.
Adam Lindsay Gordon, "The Swimmer"
set to music by Elgar in *Sea pictures*

Day after day I long
For sun-girt, sunkissed, surfing Aussie land
Would even dare the waves in Bondi Beach.
Verse Letter from John Betjeman to Norman
Williams and Patsy Zeppel, February 1963

Monday morning
Got a message —
"Gone to Bondi,
back on Sunday.
If you see me
from the beach,
be on my surf-board,
out of reach.
Gone to Bondi,
out of reach."
Bondi, Bondi,
Bondi Beach.
Oh! fierce white horses!
Bondi Beach.

Strine haiku

What a bonzer day in Broome,
riding our horses down Cable Beach.
Beaut!

Freedom

You want a kind of benevolent tyranny, then?
D. H. Lawrence, *Kangaroo*

Simple really,
as the lady said
in Adelaide,
"In spite of the cruelty to convicts,
the brutality of the military men,
in spite of all that,
once they were free
they were free.
From the mean streets of England,
they found freedom —
freedom to swim in the surf,
to gallop in the bush,
to breathe the fresh air,
to feel the warm sun
and to flourish."
There is still a problem
for deconstruction.
One man's freedom
is another man's fetters,
and even out here

in the classless society
they have tugged their forelocks
to their "betters" or worse.
Newer Australians
can blame the first British.
They feel free
not to share the guilt
in the Museum of Migration,
in the Tasmanian Museum
of Aboriginal Life.
History can be very (in)convenient.
The captions tell us what to think.

> *Heave away.*
> *Haul away.*

Strange fauna at Uluru
(Ayers Rock)

Bipeds with tripods: strange fauna seen climbing.
It's thirty-nine degrees today.
Desert oaks and spinifex,
red sand and purple parakeelya
— flora more fitting.

A helicopter on Uluru.
The flying doctor must be at hand.
Rangers with ropes,
paramedics to the rescue.
A tourist fell from the sacred rock.
He broke his fall on a lower ledge.
Fifty metres from the top.
He'd been warned by Anangu
not to try the climb.
We have all been warned.
Some show respect, look up and wonder.
Strange fauna
lying injured,
trapped in a gully.

Frail fauna at the Olgas:
dehydrated tourists fall
with heat-stress, heat-stroke.
Again the flying doctor comes.

Slowly, slowly, the sun goes down.
Uluru is left alone.
Pale misty lilac.
Rich rusty brown.

Ficus benghalensis

A sacred tree,
Ficus benghalensis.
Brahma lives there.
Ficus benghalensis.
Friend of possums
and of birds.
We admire its roots
which dangle down.
The Hindu merchants'
banyan fig tree:
they set their stalls
beneath its shade.
Ficus benghalensis.
Brahman fig-tree —
stretching out tentacles
to take us, entangled.

Silversides, Bermuda

The water explodes
in a circle of slaughter:
a shoal of small fry.

A flash of tails,
a flurry of fins:
the predators rush at their prey.

The jacks and mackerel
snap up the minnows:
a wild bubbling cauldron.

Bermuda

I spent a week in Fairyland
and slept on pink and golden sand
surrounded by the coral sea.
Soon the tempest came
and took control,
left deep disquiet in my soul.

Bermuda haiku

Too much beauty in one small place.
Near perfection.
I must get away.

Blossom time, Washington DC

> Loveliest of trees, the cherry . . .
> A. E. Housman, *A Shropshire Lad*

Is a single tree in bloom enough —
or should one seek a thousand?
A sea of trees transforms the mindscape —
who is Zen enough for one?

Blue Ridge Mountains

Blue Ridge Mountains horseback ride;
down the forest track in Fall.
The owl is watching. The coyote prowls.
The deer are grazing; quilts are stitched
in the Shenandoah Valley.
Country singers entertain us:
Bluegrass or Nashville, they glorify war.

Noah's harp
For Noah Lewis, Blues harmonica player (1895-1961)

The cries of animals excluded,
drowning in the rising flood.
Prisoners' wails,
freight trains heading north.

Frost-bitten feet,
nose frozen to mouth-harp.

A crime against humanity —
Don't say we weren't warned

Lead in air, soil and water,
mercury in river and sea.
If I don't have a headful of lead,
God knows where the metals may be.

Hormones in the meat,
chemicals in the food;
I am what I eat.
What I cannot excrete
may poison my blood
or cripple my feet.
The food chain ends with me.

Industrial discharge and effluents,
sewage and oil slicks at sea.
Nuclear waste for good measure.
When you grow up, what do *you* want to be?

Cities unfit for habitation.
The government helps to poison the nation.

"My violent behaviour and psychosis
is a direct result,
of the air I breathed as a child.
Or it could be the result
of the air my mother used to breathe . . .
I plead diminished responsibility, Your Honour."

Beware contaminated fish!
Beware the solder inside tin cans!
Beware water which flows through pipes of lead!
Beware the dust from asbestos sheets!

Beware roadside particle pollution!
Beware the fumes from car exhausts,
CO_2 from coal-fired power stations!
Beware the smoke from cigarettes!
Beware the paint that flakes from walls!
Beware insecticides, aerosol sprays,
methyls, ethyls and poisonous nitrates!

Disablement, brain damage, blood disorders,
toxic symptoms and chronic effects.
Remember, remember, Minamata.
Refuse to forget all those who've died.

To those who reject the findings
    of unbiased scientific research:
          Anathema!
To those who distort and misrepresent
    the established facts to further their own selfish ends:
          Anathema!
To those who profiteer and speculate, pollute and exploit,
    who protect their revenue rather than the environment
    and the health of all our children:
          Anathema!
To those who suppress vital information
    when it is in the public interest
    that it should be broadcast daily:
          Anathema!
To those who protect the status quo
    rather than recognise our right to know:
          Anathema!
             Anathema!
                Anathema!

Hyacinthus orientalis

You forced your way out
so Apollo could see you
between the old flagstones
paving our yard.

Born once again
from the blood you once shed
your sweet-perfumed florets
trumpet such scent!

Beloved of Apollo,
of Zephyr, the West Wind,
wild oriental,
Hyakinthos lives!

Delphic Oracle

Go tell the King:
The water that spoke has been silenced.

Go tell the King:
The wine that once spoke has turned bitter.

Go tell the King:
The birds that once sang have migrated,
all of them now flock together,
eagles and doves are now brothers.

Go tell the King:
Jackdaws preside in the palace
under the eyes of invisible vultures.

Go tell the King:
Far-off the birdsong is building,
talons and beaks are being sharpened.

Go tell the King:
The palace will crumble in ruins
and no one will ever rebuild it.

Go tell the King these things.

Lightning Source UK Ltd.
Milton Keynes UK
UKHW010219140121
376750UK00001B/9